IT WAS NEVER GOING TO BE OKAY

it was never going to be okay

jaye simpson

NIGHTWOOD EDITIONS

2020

Nightwood Editions
P.O. Box 1779
Gibsons, BC VON 1VO
Canada
www.nightwoodeditions.com

COVER DESIGN: Angela Yen
TYPESETTING: Carleton Wilson

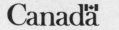

Nightwood Editions acknowledges the support of the Canada Council for the Arts, the Government of Canada, and the Province of British Columbia through the BC Arts Council.

This book has been produced on 100% post-consumer recycled, ancient-forest-free paper, processed chlorine-free and printed with vegetable-based dyes.

Printed and bound in Canada.

LIBRARY AND ARCHIVES CANADA CATALOGUING IN PUBLICATION

Title: It was never going to be okay / by jaye simpson.
Names: simpson, jaye, author.
Description: Poems.
Identifiers: Canadiana (print) 20200213679 | Canadiana (ebook) 20200213687 |
ISBN 9780889713826 (softcover) | ISBN 9780889713833 (ebook)
Classification: LCC PS8637.I4863 I89 2020 | DDC C811/.6—dc23

For all the queer NDN foster kids out there.

contents

ONE

TWO

THREE

FOUR

let me be clear: any love I find will be treason

– Hieu Minh Nguyen

I'll sing to you until you sing back

– Leanne Betasamosake Simpson

ONE

sea glass

call me sea glass:
    found after a dreamy   hot   day,
        beachside stomach full of fruit,
               skin kissed by the sun.

    call me sea glass:
        smooth around the edges
           just the right amount of
               opaque, clear & cloudy.

    call me sea glass:
               auntie loved it,
               had me framed in mosaic
                   above her fireplace,
                      wind   chimes
          of me singing
               through coastal wind.

    call me sea glass:
        because i once was sharp
           broken   tossed   in
                     tumultuous   tides
     thrashed on barnacle-   &   coral-clad rock,
pitched on log after drunken sunset
    witnessed by shifting bonfire light.

    they hardly ever remember

                                 i used to cut.

they forget

that in order to love me:

i had to break,
smashed apart.

i held poison,
dripped venom on flesh,
                kissed on the lips
                        straight out of the bottle.

how often you find me
                smooth & soft
                after being torn through
                        countless   grains   of   trauma;

coping:

you like me only then.

only when i am smooth
        around the edges,
                when i am the perfect amount
                                of opaque,
        when i am wound in copper
                laid   upon   your chest.

when i am wind chimes & picture frames & after i can no longer cut.

call me sea glass
        because you can only
                love me

when i'm broken   &   small   &   harmless.

    call me sea glass
        found on the shore,
            foamy salt waves lapping
                at my edges, you find me:

                                      beautiful.

teeth & sharp bones (a dialogue)

some of us had lived long enough
to think that we had made it out:
      so some of us decided to start a new
      love again, try   &   bring fire back
      into this world.

what we didn't expect
    was to be burying
        our own children,
because when they entered
the world of the living—
    we thought we had
        truly made it out alive.

    yet still they hold these babies accountable
for the *sins of our ancestors*,
  let's get something straight for once:

we didn't commit any sin.

unless you count breathing as sin.
  so i guess that john a. macdonald wanted us dead
    was sin enough.

ᐧᐧᐧᐧᐧᐧᐧ /\/\/\/\/\/\/\

when i was a child
    you took me from my mother,
      you said she didn't know how to be one,
        you stole her mother & her mother's mother before her,
        gave us to white women wolves

& got mad at us for having teeth
& sharp bones.

of course we'd have edges & sharpness
　　what did you expect when
　　　　the white women wolves decided
　　　　　　they were hungry for a little
　　　　　　　　more than some quick income every month:

　　　　　　they'd sink their teeth into our soft flesh,
carve contemporary runes of colonization & abuse into our　　bones.

don't get mad at my teeth & sharp edges;
　　　　　　　　even after moving
　　　　　　　　　　　　mountains　　&　　oceans
　　　　　　　　　　　　　　　i couldn't stop this—
　　　　　　　　　　　　　couldn't change this cycle
　　　　　　　　　　　　　　　in its tracks:
　　even i, all fire & flood bloodline
　　　　　　& bloodlust couldn't stop
　　　　　　　　these colonial governments
　　　　　　　　　　from trying to steal my kin.

ΛΛΛΛΛΛΛΛ

　　　　　　　　i've buried too many of my cousins and
　　　　　　　　　　now i'm burying their children too;
　　　　　　　　　　　don't think this anything new.
you call us bad parents
　　fail to recognize
　　　　you stole our parents
　　　　　　the moment they were born—
　　　　　　　　& you call their parents bad parents

again, fail to recognize
   you also stole their parents
      when they were born,
         hell, you stole their parent's parents
            when they were children,

trying to flee
   from white men & women
      adorned in red and black.

/\/\/\/\/\/\/\

some of us lived long enough
   to think we made it out:
      & now we're burying our own children
         & they're burying us too.

don't dare think
   this cycle ended with me
      i couldn't stop it.

                    you call us dangerous
                       when you took
                       away all our weapons
                    except our teeth   &   bones
                       & now you're upset
                       your flesh got caught
                       on the sharp edges.

                       why were you there
                          in the first place?

boy

i am eight & my foster father lets me read in his library,

the piano mournfully sings mozart & i am under it hiding from my siblings' cruel laughter & delight. as i am reading about edgar cayce, atlantis, the sahara & the fall of rome, c s lewis' science fiction. peter says:

>   *stay here*
>   *you are safe here*

i am seven, & my sisters are painting their nails. shiny with clear coat over pastels. they have locked me in the laundry room, i can hear their giggling

the lights are off &
i am crying again & by again
i mean i am laying on the floor trying to see them from the space between the door & floor.
                   the linoleum is stripped from my salt-heavy tears and rushed breath. i have been doing this for years.

i am five
my sisters are saying *boy*
i do not know what the word means but
i am bruised into knowing it: the blunt *b*,
the hollowness of the *o*, the blade of *y*
oh how they struck

                   struck when i stole a doll

                   brushed her hair & changed her outfit,
                   saying to myself: *i want to be painted*
                   nails, long locks of shiny hair & soft.

17

my foster mother, a cold rock of a mountain, temperamental & prone to
avalanches overhears *painted nails, long locks, soft*. not *boy*.
she cascades and i am pushed out from under the bed, dragged by my ear by
her gravity and i am forced
to stand naked. struck as she yells
boy.

i am eight,

i am in the mirror looking at my naked
    body. i have been doing this for years:
    pushing prepubescent fat together. i am eight
    i am crying at the hairdresser's as my sisters are treated like goddesses,
preened while i am pruned.

i am crying,
called   *fag*   for the first time, soon my classmates are saying it, asking
me if i am gay & running   as if i am contagious, as if they are at risk,
as if this was something you could get in the stalls of the boys' washroom.

boy.

        i am boy in mother's house.
        bound to the blunt *b*,
        the hollowness of *o*,
        the blade of *y*

except in father's favourite room, where i am free to just be, reading while the
piano mournfully sings mozart and i am under it hiding from my siblings.
crying as peter says, *stay here you are safe here*

peter,
when the piano stopped playing mozart and just became silent in your absence,
the library was converted into a mausoleum
i was left with only words. I miss the sound of the piano, the times we spent in the
garden,
you loved the rhododendrons & roses,
the strawberries & rhubarb. peter, you had a box of seeds in the shed, picked one
at random and planted it. the spring after you died, you must've known for the
only seeds left were forget-me-nots.
peter, you understood me like you knew the way the piano keys made noise, the
way a plant grows from seed to flower. i had to mourn well after you'd left.

      i am nine, i am crying
    you are dead & i am boy
   now boy because i do not want
    boy because they are watching,
    boy because they say

they never asked me if i was, only told me i was,
& i was not

     the blunt *b*,   the hollowness of *o*,   or the blade of *y*.

haunting (a poem in six parts)

i. the family photo albums

have you haunted photo albums before?
        been the blurry phantom in the background?
                a sorrowful spectre?

    i was taught by wooden spoon
        that children were seen & not heard;
        my pale flesh must've been reminder
                that i was burden & beast
                all in one.

taught to be ghost   long   before
        i could wrap my own hands around
                my throat—
        spoke to spirits long before
         i realized i was just as dead
                as they were.

ii. wrong kind of indian

i sometimes dream of curried goat
               & the cast iron flat pan
                    cynthia would use to fry roti.
                          she would wet the bottom
                          of a red enamel mug
                          to spread oil before frying (one time she
laughed when i asked if i could flip the roti. she laughed even harder when
i asked for the recipe. said i was the wrong kind of indian for roti. said i was
the wrong kind of brown, too white for my own. said i had a cleaner getaway
than my cousins).

             i was too young to understand.

     my fingers were always yellow after
     my nails a deep hue of spice.
     after peter died, she cooked less.

                    told me feed myself,
                         that now was a good time
                                    to learn.

iii. the family photo albums 2

one year, i came across
        a family album:
                couldn't find a smaller version
of myself
                couldn't find a fuller smile
of myself
                couldn't find anything
but photos
                of a woman i called cynthia,
a dead man & their daughter.
            i saw vacations
                in disneyland, mexico & london
                (ones i was always kept from)

iv. thieving intentions

remember how she told me
    not to ever call her momma,
               grandma
                   or auntie.
when she felt generous
        or
         i cried too much:
    she'd chuckle and ask if i needed
    some of her good old TLC
    (t e n d e r l o v i n' c a r e).

        sometimes if i plucked enough slugs

        from the strawberry patches,

        or gardened enough,

        especially after peter died,

      she'd let me rest my head

    on her chest. The sound of her

    breathing felt like i was stealing

s   o   m   e   t   h   i   n   g

                    not for me.

                        i stopped
            reaching   out
        when she   locked the door
        to my   bedroom,
            got used   to wet pillows
                        from crying,
                        stopped trying
                        to impress
                        her, stopped
                        doing
                        homework
                        stopped
                        laughing
                        stopped
                        painting
                        & drawing
                        stopped writing
                        & started reading, ran away
                        to the library
                        made sanctuary between
                        shelves
                        & book covers
                        learned to stop asking

vi. the cost of a photograph

one　　　　christmas
　　　　　　　after living
　　　　　　　　　in her home for near a decade
　　　　during a large dinner
　　　　　with her extended relatives:

　　　　　someone called for a family photo.

　　　　　　　　i went to take my place in it
　　　　she said *this one's for family*—
　　　swatting my sister & me away.
　　the camera caught
the blur of my back.
　　it is the only family photo i am in.

have you haunted photo albums before?

00088614   /why/   00088614/00088614/00088614/00088614
    00088614/0088614/00088614000886140008861400088614
/00088614000886140008861400088614000886140008861400088614000886140008
8614000886140008861400088614000886140008861400088614000886140008861400
08861400088614/00088614
    /didn't/   00088614000886140008861400088614   /you/
    00088614000886140008861400088614000886140008861400088614000886140
08861400088614000886140008861400088614/00088614000886140008861
40008861400088614000886140008861400088614000886140008861400088614000886
14000886140008861400088614000886140008861400088614000886140008861400
088614000886140008861400088614000886140008861400088614
/00088614000886140008861400088614000886140008861400088614000886140008
8614000886140008861400088614000886140008861400088614000886140008861400
08861400088614/00088614000886140008861400088614000886140008861400088614000886140008861
40008861400088614000886140008861400088614000886140008861400088614000886140008
861400088614000886140008861400088614000886140008861400088614   /say/
00088614000886140008861400088614000886140008861400088614000886140008861400088
614000886140008861400088614000886140008861400088614000886140008861400088614000
88614000886140008861400088614000886140008861400088614000886140008861400088614000886140
00886140008861400088614000886140008861400088614000886140008861400088614000886140008861
40008861400088614000886140008861400088614000886140008861400088614/00088614000
8861400088614000886140008861400088614000886140008861400088614000886140008861400088614
0008861400088614000886140008861400088614000886140008861400088614000886140008861
40008861400088614000886140008861400088614/00088614000
8861400088614000886140008861400088614000886140008861400088614000886140008861400088614000886140008861400088614
00088614

    000886140008861400088614000886140008861400088614000886140008861400
0886140008861400088614000886140008861400088614/000886140008861
40008861400088614000886140008861400088614000886140008861400088614000886140008
861400088614000886140008861400088614
/my/   00088614000886140008861400088614
000886140008861400088614000886140008861400088614000886140008861400088
614000886140008861400088614000886140008861400088614000886140008861400088614000

88614000886140008861400088614000886140008861400088614000886140
00886140008861400088614000886140008861400088614000886140008861
40008861400088614000886140008861400088614000886140008861400088
614000886140008861400088614000886140008861400088614000886140008
861400088614000886140008861400088614000886140008861400088614000
08861400088614000886140008861400088614000886140008861400088614
000886140008861400088614000886140008861400088614000886140008861
61400088614000886140008861400088614000886140008861400088614000
88614000886140008861400088614000886140008861400088614000886140
00886140008861400088614000886140008861400088614000886140008861400088614000886
14
00088614

/name?/

her. (i.)

dissociation   &   i
       became sweethearts in grade eight
we'd meet in the morning before first period,
linger between library shelves during lunch
   &   part just before falling asleep.

dissociation   &   i
   the sweetest relationship
      throughout it all, didn't know you could be co-
      dependent with loneliness
wouldn't have called this coping.

how desperate i was:
   mother #4 taught me any touch was attention enough,
     any inclination a gift
      for troubled kids like me.

dissociation   &   i
       split:
     to not feel doesn't mean it didn't happen.

her. (ii.)

i've let her inside—
    over   steeping:
burnt jasmine
    white tea.

no honey
      nor bandage
could hide
      this wound,
          justified as
      bloodletting.

arnica personified
    seeps into vein,
         membrane,   organ   &   muscle
  flushed   &   failing.

still my tongue
    craves the souring
          bleeding
            faltering heartbeat.

i have swallowed
    wildfire flame,
      arnica cordifolia,
pleaded for her to leave these hollowing bones—
    bit off more than i could chew
      bled out forgetting
        that i was the one
          who opened the door.

metal // biting down // i

metal as in   biting tongue to keep silent

       as in   copper,   red rust between   yellowing ivory

       as in

                         breaking skin.

metal as in   bent

       as in   pushed between two stronger objects

       as in   purposefully adding trauma to bend something.

metal as in   i

       as in   this body bending   &   twisting

       as in   breaking when the trauma applied

                         is too much too soon.

       as in

                         mined, melted down   &   forged.

metal as in   copper in blood

                         holding this tongue,

                            biting down has always been

                                    first response.

biting down as in   leather clenched between teeth

           as in   tearing flesh off bone

           as in   shutting this damn mouth.

metal as in   biting down.

biting down as in   metal.

                         when i speak i often bleed.

TWO

nogojiwanong // peterborough

lavender shortbread dipped in   london fog   foam
    a quaint café appropriately named   *black honey*
    in nogojiwanong // peterborough
        a rainy day signalled the end of my time here.

i had come to realize many things:
    that i loved too deeply
        too ferociously
            too hard   &   that i fell too often.

that tiptoe touch-and-go love affair
(& i use the word affair because that's what it felt like):
    had been built on too many *maybe*s
       &   *possibly*s   &   *i'm confused*s.
indecisiveness a fog
        of uncertainty   &   at times i felt
left in the dark   &   you embarrassed to
           have even had feelings for me.
you said
    i like the distance
       between us:
&   how just
    before you
      said that
        i had wanted to shorten
         the distance between
you   &   i.

i was   &   still am
fault lines   &   fallen leaves
fragments   &   fissures:

placed too much ideation in another,
     hoped to be whatever you wanted
        didn't listen when i wasn't what you were looking for
        &   blamed you for it.
     wrong of me to ask you to want me // still i faulted you
        the sapphic poets didn't teach
     how to be accountable
        when yearning.

to be upfront is a gambit;
     want to be touched
      when the sun shone
        on my face just right,
          after having just swum in the pacific,
         brine making my skin
           salty   &   hair curly:
the good kind of salt
   &   to feel like that
        instead of licking up sulphur
          from mother #4's garden.

     you didn't know me
        in mine:
between the strawberries   &   rhubarb
   by the thyme   &   golden sage
                &   salem's rosemary
right by the cardamom plant   &   basil
when i was happier with what was   &   what wasn't.

never told you what i wanted
     prayed you'd tell me you wanted more,
        that i know how to perform.

cruel the affection,
 severe the incision   &   jealousy was never a good look on me.

lavender shortbread dipped in   london fog   foam
 a quaint café appropriately named *black honey,*
 this ruin my design.

the end of a friendship

after florence + the machine's "big god"

i hope this sacrifice led you to believe again
　　　　　my blood pooling
　　　　　at your feet
　　　　　will water
　　　　your gardens for years to come:

　　　　　　　　　this hallowed cost was more than enough.

i hope my sacrifice kept the gods　　　　　above appeased,
　　　　you get to go on　　&　　love each other
　　　　　this was *always* meant to be a polyamorous tragedy
　　　　　　　　& i was *always* meant to play this part,
typecast in my manifestation—
　　　　　　　my final bow crowned with thistled tribulation.

i have been the favourite spectre of so many:
　　　　　knowing how to wail & cry
　　　　　　　whilst gliding through these　　　red velour hallways,
i have always known how to keen & quake in synchronous perfection.
　　　　　　　isn't this what filled the seats in the first place?

you were always meant to make it in the next saga &
　　　i was destined to exit stage left for your character development.

　　　　　jesus christ, jesus christ it hurts.

you always to get the favour of my sacrifice,
　　　　　　　benefit from this price paid.
　　　　　　　this wasn't always about you:

it was about this burning heavenly heart i had to cut out.
let that be the final curtain call,   no standing ovation in the final act.
let this be the way i go,   this sacrifice not be in vain
                            nor was it for you either;
               hearts often do belong nailed to crosses now.

        as i turn putrid in the unrelenting sun
which beats upon my downturned brow
      you *finally* think of laying me to rest:
please drive a coffin nail into my left hand
               & place labradorite in my right,
fill my sallow chest   with wild stra wberry & rose plants,
       cover my eyes with prairie wildfire,
lay seneca root at my feet,
                    let me face east
& do not let me burn for too long.

      jesus christ, jesus christ this hurts.

inheritance

i have my father's hands
      wide   &   unforgiving
never knowing
      strength to hold on tight enough—
sometimes the only inheritance
      a child gets is the reminder
            of how unwanted they were,
                        features left
                    only to haunt.

i have my mother's smile
                wide   &   unwavering
knowing all too well
      the end in the beginning—
loving the idea of someone so much
                she passed
                  on to me
      this legacy of longing.

i know my father
      through grainy facebook photo,
cursor hovering
      over send

      how would he react
        to a daughter with his hands?

he wanted his ill-begotten son
      to learn how to   snare   &   hunt   &   trap
now he's got a child called   trap   &   trick.

i am pieces of them
      flesh   &   bone,
their tragedy.

i, child made folly:

     what parts of me are mine
if i am still scared of an absentee father's opinion.

//

came back in pieces

what have you done?

came back in pieces

where did you go?

came back in pieces

when did this happen?

named every crack & fault line
    cried   out   to   them
told you when the break
                 //
                   broke open,
how much inside came outside—
            called it fun
            called it family
            called it anything to justify the means.

came back with barely enough
        to know it was me,
        grew comfortable
            in the quiet between what was left
        & what was taken.

i
        can't recall
when i wasn't.

this woman //nookum

to irene

how do i explain my queerness to the gatekeeper of my bloodline
        when she flushed hers out with communion wine
                                                &   holy water?
        how do i explain my ever-shifting body to the woman who prayed for
my damnation, rather than my absolution?
        my grandmother who held me at birth,   has prayed for my end
more than my success,   she'd done this many times over,
        begging god that we'd be better off dead,   burying two-spirit
cousin after two-spirit cousin—
        hanging their queer bodies
                like a slaughtered coyote on a post
                        as to say, *do not come around here no more.*

this woman
        does not see the two-spirit as hallowed or sacred,
but sees me as crawling out of the mud like a demon
        to bring forth the end of the world,
                the four-headed beast of revelations.

this woman
        cut down the family tree to build the church
                                where our funerals would be.

this woman
        salted the fields where we were meant to grow.

this woman
        was never taught how to love.

41

this woman
            begged for residential school,   etched colonization into
her bones,   cracked into marrow to write passages
            out of the bible in her right hand in white-blood-cell matter.

this woman
            broke the bible on my mother's back,
            bruised   &   branded old testament unto softer flesh,
tried to exorcise intergenerational trauma as if it was some demon.

but holy water does not wine make;
            this woman
                        granted herself absolution
                                    with the blood of christ
                                                &   holy water.

this woman
            buried my mother in the colonizer's church,
            cut my hair the night before
                        told me to say my prayers or i'd end up in hell
                                    with my mother.
                        told me to be a *good indian, do not cry.*

            i would rather outlive her now than explain my queerness,
            know how she'd already cast me out,
            strike my back raw,   rip my claim from my mother tongue,
                        flay me in front of the land that birthed our people.

this woman
            cut down the family tree to build the church
                                                where our funerals would be.

this woman
    would rather an empty church,
        a graveyard full of her children
            than actually know who we were.

urban NDNs in the DTES

had a dozen foster parents
                    tell me to run from my mother's truth
                    the track marks up her arm,
                    shy away from the streets
                                        they said ate her alive.

            wasn't until i had rewilded
                    unto the very streets
                            that i recognized that it kept her alive.

harm came from
            the môniyâw men
                    lurking in the alleys asking for something more
(like ligament or limb)
            wrap their fleshy
                    digits around ikwe throat
squeeze life like pressing
            orange for juice.

most of my mom's sisters are dead
                                        like her too now—
                    caught in the crosshairs
                            of murdered or missing;
their children are working
            & i make sure to say hello to my cousins,
                    we all picked up our mothers'
                    work eventually.

i have become a regular at the funeral parlour on hastings.
burying parent & child every other week.

don't have tears left once home, save them

                                   for longer nights
remember there are NDN children
who need to eat still.

i ran onto main and hastings
cried out in anguish, this place called cold
                         called heartless
                         called monster & maw
was never the culprit & the blame was never to be
my mother's or her sisters'—
                    rather machines of genocide
                         placed here by
                         the illegal government voted in
                         by our now-neighbours.

i've found truth:
        the mythos was fabricated;
& there will always be
funerals to attend,
NDN children to feed.

it is too late:

dispersion settles in the unsettled
                                    amongst children
born into unknowing

                    if the flora can speak
                    the same tongue.

can the stunted birch
                        at trout lake park
                        speak nêhinawêwin
                        or anishinaabemowin
the way the skyward birch
                        with prairie storm sing
                        to pickerel &
                        amik in skownan?

            maybe you can
relearn//unlearn
            the feeling
            of nimama
pulled from throat,
            flayed tongue worn
on nun's habit
            three matriarchs
back?

do you think they too are eavesdropping?
                            (our ancestors i mean)
do you think they understand
                        why their kin speak
                        their abusers' language?

i think they understand enough
        when i cry out for home//land—
desperate in this diaspora: ravenous
                to belong to a before.

flinch

all of my lovers have flinched from my touch, or flinched from their own touch, them touching me. i am the monster from under the bed or the back of the closet, but does that mean touch is worth the flinch? i flinch too. usually away because i want to run, i want to escape, as touch has never been safe before now—it has always been a strike or a blow or a kick or a punch and now it feels similar. i am human still, yet all my lovers have flinched from my touch, and all of my lovers have flinched touching me, and i notice. i do not think some try to hide it, but those who do are worse. they touch still, and i see the fleeting sneer and upraised brow, i am undesirable on that front, so many have used me to keep them warm at night, so many have used me to feel, how often i am used. slaying the beast, a side quest complete, and yet still they flinch and i flinch and i do not want to be touched anymore and i still want to be touched. i am scared of wanting this and not wanting this so often that if i could take a pill to stop wanting touch, i would.

but here we are, under rainy streetlights, ambling toward fleeting moments of desperate touch and feeling. at this point i expect the flinch, i am ready for it, i am prepared to lose, i am prepared to be touched with the lights off. that still doesn't make it easier, the flinch, the recoil from something meant to be sacred. this isn't easy, it won't be and i know it will never be easy. the flinch and i, we are in the longest relationship outside of dissociation, a sickened polyamorous relationship of primal physical reactions and coping mechanisms. i still long for it though, not the flinch, but the thing that causes it: touch. i want touch that isn't born of fetishization or desperation, i want touch born of healthy intentions, sure and full of consent. i do not want touch purely because of my fatness, nor my transness. i want touch because someone wants to hold *me* and because i am *me*. touch me because you want to touch me, not because you feel like you have to, touch me because it is something we both want.

loving in the dark

after amy winehouse's "tears dry on their own"

loving in the dark
        has been my specialty for as long
                as i can remember:
lost count of all the lovers
        who decided my skin was only
             to be touched with lights off.

i have gotten so used to the shadows,
fleeting   &   fleeing from the light,
        ghosts of our passion,
              my hubris
                    their fetish.
desire   &   lust
                        kept us there,
                 by great design.

so used to loving
        in the dark,   though by definition
        it is not love,   just a bastardization of stolen
           intentions   &   longings painted on chapped lips
          tied between sharp teeth.

        no love in
            touching after the blinds
                have been drawn, lights dimmed
        never seeing their faces
                   //   still   //

i answer the door:
        they, quick to leave
               i, a shipwreck
in my own bed,   in my own sheets,
    the ocean spilling out across the crinkled linens.

the dark
        hasn't left me in such precarious standing:
          what men do   in the dark has.

how can i love in the light?
        i cry when i ask the question
          that will end this torrid love affair:

                                do you love me?

quick to leave,
        salt water leaking as my voice trembles,
          will this be any easier in the day?
                  with the lights on?
                      outside?

will you tell me you love me?
clothes on,   curtains   &   blinds open,
                    lights on love me?
will i love you
clothes on,   curtains   &   blinds open,
                    lights on love you?

pattern decrees i will cry
        after every touch
          after every word
            after every breath.

loving in the dark
    has been my specialty for as long
        as i can remember:
           crying while doing so
               has been my specialty for just as long too.

head & heart & hands & health (a poem in four parts)

i. head

i pledge my head to clearer thinking…

i now only come to visit for weddings, funerals & holidays—occasionally to fuck those who were too scared to come out in my grad year or the boys who are now fathers.

i remember when my closest high school girlfriends decided to take me, one of the school's resident losers, for our school's grad kidnapping. dressing me up as a girl was tradition, whilst they had taped a two-litre bottle of cheap cider to my hand & got me drunk for the first time. oddly enough, i am still friends with them even though one of them got married & never invited me.

i ended up getting roofied & spent the night tied to a lawn chair crying while my grad year partied. one of the juiceheads knocked the teeth out of the head of some girl's boyfriend from another school & he nearly lost his US football scholarships but being the son of the sheriff came with perks.

i never wanted to drink in the bushes after that. getting drugged in the woods does that to you.

ii. heart

i pledge my heart to greater loyalty...

a friend of the family scribbled *if only my girlfriend was this dirty* on his suv after my brother's funeral. i think my brother would laugh at that. i light my fifth clove cigarette of the day & inhale. fiddle with my knit winter jacket. step from foot to foot.

later that day "jackson" plays overhead in the small shop & i think of how old country music makes me move: a good banjo & fiddle. i decide not to steal, none of their rings are silver & i think gold looks cheap.

the white hipster busker on victoria & fourth is singing "hotel california" while playing an acoustic guitar missing a string or two & i see the café who protected an abuser has closed down. that happens here, the country bump-kin white whisper network is treacherous between the church pews & the red barn aisles where i bought tack.

i hold my tongue here more. i have no stake in a place that would rather carve my heart out for existing than let me live as me. my heart has long left like some cliché young ingenue arriving in a big city (à la rachel berry in *glee*). four summers ago, in a mcdonald's, at two in the morning a woman calls me a tranny for wearing red revlon liquid lipstick.

iii. hands

i pledge my hands to greater service…

parents #4 & #5 didn't realize i wanted to be in 4-H so i could dreamily stare at boys. something about cowboys did something to me: my first crush was a blond boy in a rival 4-H club. plus free tickets to the pacific national exhibition was a win back then.

i sometimes let rougher hands hold me down, in back seats of lifted trucks on quiet logging roads that mar the scraggly desert forest. a man died a few years back on these roads & a black bear had gorged herself on the putrid flesh until someone found him.

a stifling summer some millennia ago, a cute dusty blond boy lets his hand linger on my back, winks & gestures to the showers above the stadium. panic had made home in my stomach. this could end with broken bones or a silence i would not be able to handle. i do not follow him.

now hungrier hands pull hair & limb, exhaust patience while fucking up pronouns. my stepsister says the neighbourhood in vancouver i live in is full of trannies while smoking outside the funeral home. i inhale the last of my illegal clove cigarette, dial a cab while flicking the butt into a nearby can.

iv. health

i pledge my health to better living…

i better not fucking die here.

THREE

fever

a   space

        not yet hollowed // hallowed
             still

                                    ghost limb:
all wet // full of longing
        so much so i refuse to name it

                              lust

my wildest dreams
        pressed
          against bladder.

i am no eileithyia
      &   i will usher in no child from mine;
not to be mother
        only wombless maiden
never make it to crone
     no godhood in triplicate:
         a garden of ephemeral flowers
         i am no fruit-bearing tree.

many tomorrows from now i pray
        my bed full of babies
                        warm   &   chubby
are held in arms
        that understand there are NDN babies
          who will want me
          as much as i want them

norman fucking rockwell! is lana del rey's greatest album

unsatisfied with his consumption,
             a white man left bruises & blood
                      bodies like mine are ones he fills up
                         with what he thinks his manhood is.

he, grappling at the expanse of me
             clawing at edges—trying to tear
pieces of flesh,
                marks on my left breast
                      where he clings.

i ask   if men like him
bury seed in both cis & trans women;
             men like him don't always answer with
she knows i like trans girls too.

(i wish he ends the sentence with a period.
but he leaves that open like wound
like womb.)

we fuck on the bed they both own,
             my red hair, her white pillow
                       & still he watches—
all desire & lust, hungrier mouth asking
                           if i wanted to be bent.

instead i steel myself
                as he finishes loudly.

i am the flesh at the end of him
when she leaves town,
i am bruised breasts & bitten lips
purple & red
unsatisfied with being consumed.

bedroom hymns

after florence + the machine's "bedroom hymns"

i wish deeply
that i could've written
"bedroom hymns" about you:
    you a holy rite
        a body & love,
            my selfish prayers
              of not getting enough.

another trans woman warns
there may be a chance
that a cis man will hurt me:
fall prey to his consumption,
intoxicated by what i freely
give to him.

                    (i warn myself:
                    i don't even let clients
                    lick me up so feverishly.)

we turned the couch
into an altar of sacred touch,
i, remembering how evan ducharme
& tenille campbell told me *sex is medicine*,
allow you to sweat out your confessions
on my confusing breast.
                (allow your soft lips
                to surround my swollen nipples.)

this,
your body   &   love
such selfish prayers intoxicating
with each rushed breath, each ragged intake,
each prayer moaned aloud.
          i can't get enough
          sex as medicine
          (his scrunched-up face)
          a cacophony of ecstasy:
          jesus on his breath
i ache out onto him—
his teeth grazing over
every soft & sore spot,
this narrow-hipped boy
holds me down on our shared altar.

          i brace myself on his forearms
          he kisses me deep mid-moan,
          tasting of our confessions
          i am scared he may take too much,
          desecrate this hallowed touch.

                    (there is a moment:
                    of wanting.
                    of curiosity.
                    of wishing.
                    /he lowers himself
                    asks if he can try something/
                    my breath terrifyingly rapid—
                    not ready.
                    not wanting.
                    not capable.)

he stops.

tells me
this is my body,
my choice: he raises himself
asks if i was okay,
if i wanted to keep going,
asks again if i'm okay,
tells me this is my altar first,
his last.

i am holy rite
a body   &   love,
his selfish prayers
of never getting enough:

i let your teeth carve concentric circles
around our pooling sheets,
sweat as wine   &   ritual
aching arching confessions
oh—   oh—   oh—   oh—
hecate,   persephone,   artemis   &   eris

on my breath—
you turn me into moonlight
whilst we grapple
to get closer to each other.

in a city without seasons ...

after florence + the machine's "sky full of song"

⌂ *... it keeps raining in* LA,
  another white boy on tinder
    tells me i look incredible in
      every single one of my photos.

🌴. attempting to be orpheus,
  i do not want to be eurydice,
    i fear i will be at the end of this.

🧑. four months later
 orpheus sings me a song
  in his bedroom
   about feeling undeserving
    of affection & love,
     turning me into dust
      on many couches
       & many beds.

⚠. shame follows attraction
  to whomever's gaze
   falls upon this body:
    turns their dicks to stone
     & shortly after
      their hearts.

😿. i feel like a collision
        of grecian warnings:
                to want is deserving
                        of punishment enough
                                & i cry from burbank
                                        to little thailand
                                                from venice beach
                                                        to los feliz.

☁. *i couldn't hide*
        from the th—nder
                in a sky full of s—ng
                        & i want y—u so badly
                                but y—u could be anyone.

🕊. gather myself from dust
    hades' restitution denied
        as i climb out,
            shame forgets
                the desire to continue,
                    want for everything
                        i never had—
                                orpheus couldn't keep me.

✿. raindrops,
        obscene in their greatness
            splatter our faces, refreshing reminders
                of persephone's mercy
                    between the forever of LA,
                        city of ever-blooming flowers.

🏢. the moon,
    low-bellied at 3:12 a.m.
        as my friend & i
            are driven to LAX, shadowy palms
                in the amber haze of streetlights
                    & illuminated billboards remind me
                        desirability belongs to no one:
                            only to the ideas of people
                              we create in our head.

✈. i can always justify a reason
    to shed tears during a flight,
        be it the malleable nature
            of wanting, or the severity
                of delusion: sometimes you want
                to be wanted so badly
                    you forget yourself.

beast

pumping desire into softer flesh
                     my body, a container
                                   for all the times
man couldn't love whom he intended.

father's tongue a hatchet
clenched fist a blade
to slice up son's intimacies
(around my hips   &   throat
                           man returns his father's favours).

i have forgotten how it feels
to fall for the mythos of man
         of strong hands, of jawline

         of elbow, of crushed violet eye socket

         man will always ruin his own fabrication.

man withholds his desires
         &   destroys my sisters—
reaches for me
begs to watch me bleed in my own bedsheets
                             i run tongue across canines
                             man forgets i had a father too.

man says he isn't a fag when asking
                 to masturbate with my body.

positions
himself as conqueror, calls my body
trick,
trap,
tranny.

man fucks witch
embarrassed by his own release
the way his fingers linger   &   how he moans.
in the morning
he will tell the townspeople
she   magicked   him into wanting.

by sundown, the town centre will be awash
in the thickening red
of her burning remains.

i want to be more
than the   flesh between   man's teeth,
my skin   ribboned   by his consumption.

who is man to call me beast?

exhaustion is matted fur
gnashing teeth
blood   &   spittle
salt water   &   rippling muscles.

man forgets he is beast also.

decolonial pu$$y

i have been the storm
& the break—
the tumble
& the get back up again—
the one-time hookup
turned three-week tryst.

there isn't anything
more decolonial
than a trans woman's pu$$y.

i have been the shout
& the coarse dying cry—
i have been the blow
& the bruise—
the kiss turned
forbidden entanglement.

there is something
about the way
fucking a trans woman
sets men free.

i have been the aftermath
& the beginning—
the cliché in the hyperbole
& the metaphor in plain sight—
soft lips pulled
between his ravenous canines.

something about a cis woman
carrying child
that turns the warm between my legs
to salt, proud men tend
to bury seed in sand

pray to be fed into the fall
bite tender breast & beg for rain
by spilling our blood
as tribulation.

there ain't nothing more decolonial
than my pu$$y.

godzilla

godzilla, o
godzill a o
godz ill a ooo
gods i'll a oooo

he asks
if he can take me out
i say *the new godzilla movie*
just came out he makes a joke
about cum
i laugh, make a
mental note
to add a popcorn combo
to the deal.

in 3-D, i slip my hand in the loop
of his waistband,
tease him out: play the game.
he's cum once by the time
the white guy from
malcolm in the middle
dies twenty minutes in.

godzilla, o
godzill a o
god z i'll a oooo
god z i'll aaa o

he cries
when watanabe's
character says,
let them fight—
not for the same reason
as me:
his ex-fiancé stole
his dog & moved
to the philippines.
playing therapist again
godzilla roars in victory
this doesn't get easier,
he's no atomic breath.

godzilla, o
godzill a o

i sneak out the back after,
wait thirty minutes
go back in & purchase
another ticket
to watch godzilla

alone,

oh godzilla - ahhh.

red

he is inside
he is moving
        /fuck yeah/   –   */fuck yeah/*   –   */fuck yeah/*

i am red
he is inside
       /does it feel good?/

breathe in
       /oh babe/
breathe out

his sweat is
pabst blue ribbon
& dispensary dust,
i feel the ridged scar on his right clavicle
trace the tattoo on the lower abdomen of this narrow-hipped boy
this closeness is as near
to being wanted
as i know

       /babe does it feel good?/
not posed as a question
he strikes deep
finally *stop*
escapes my lips.

he is still inside
red outside
still trying to feel
       /oh babe/   –   */this feels good/*   –   */fuck yeah/*

let's change positions,
he is quick, hungry
he lets slip the word   */mother/*
& i am devoured

he begs for me
to slip a finger inside him
but lacked
the basic decency
to have tidied up inside.

& why let my finger smell
of shit
when he won't listen to
no.

he begs
i apathy
he begs
i become still

he is desperation
& i, necessity.

he begs
whilst inside me
still, i apathy
i am

red:
        /fuck yeah/

beautiful monsters in uncanny valley

never to be lovers jeer   &   mock
     when they hear i crush heart into powder
   lay it on altar for them

     they were told monsters cannot love
     what a show lay before them now.

i bend   &   break
     betray celestial beginnings to appease
             mortal flesh for wounding

pray tell, what do you know of betrayal?

         i have heard treacherous gospel
      when you thought i wasn't in the room,
    shocked a man like that
    would desire a beautiful monster like i.

at least you have the decency
    to acknowledge i am prettier than you.

   a week later i am called
     uncanny valley, perceived inhuman
         close but not close enough
       woman but not woman enough

full lipped   &   wound//womb -less
                  i am illusion enough for now
                                    shape-shifters are monstrous
                                    in their own
                                    infinite possibilities
                                    &   how mundane the beholder.

when the door closes   &   the light dims
        i am demure
              within these entanglements
                    far less ravenous than the mouth
                          leaving bruises carelessly.

                  &   still the treacherous gospel
                        incredulous that one would pay
                                          to bed me forgets
              there are many hungers—
                        no matter, i am not the hungry one here.

perennial love poem

my feelings are: *narcissus pseudonarcissus* & *taraxacum officinale*
    daffodils & dandelions—
yellow flowering perennials both aplenty in the dirt
      of my childhood.

daffodils die quickly, persephone's sacrifice;
        they trumpeted the end of the stolen pagan holidays:
          they heralded her triumphant return.

dandelions are one of the first things
      a pollinator chances upon after winter
         the first meal,   the breaking of the fast.

every spring he'd show me the daffodil shoots—
    his smile kind, he'd ask me to pull the weeds in their way;
daffodils couldn't save him from the disease.

she'd ask me to burn the tops of the dandelions
             to stop the spread of them,
             but when she wasn't looking
             i'd blow the seeds off, see them dance &
swirl in the breeze, they were the future & unapologetically so.

my feelings are: *narcissus pseudonarcissus* & *taraxacum officinale*
    yellow flowering perennial:
                 daffodil
    yellow flowering herbaceous perennial:
                 dandelion.

i never loved for long—

                             fleeting & far between in the fresh soil;
                             they were never mine for long either:
             disease, decay & rot
             taking place in
             tuber, bulb & root.
like the perennial—returning once again

                                     year after year;
        like the seed carried on the breeze & swirl of eddies,
                  my feelings are daffodils & dandelions.

ζήλια // jealousy

persephone: chaos bringer all of her own,
a queer delight & dismay—   yet she
    would've loved more time
with   the king of the underground,
    she would've consumed
        another six pomegranate seeds (at least).

i would've done anything
        to break such sacred fruit,
    i would've   sunk
my own ravenous teeth
    into your red betrayal
    instead tossed golden apple
            για τα πιο όμορφα
i, truly no persephone, am not to be betrothed
        to such unyielding darkness & cold:
i, truer to be chaos bringer,
    she much more to partake in my game.

eris: "goddess" of discord & strife,
    who feeds upon men
        amongst the clanging of blades
    spitting destitution into my gaping maw.

    yet still, no one has loved i,
sister of persephone: you always found the narcissus sacred
        & i too furious sacrilege.

persephone, always pitied
in her own descension,
     still: i, the one blamed,
     yes, this mess is mine.

    she far   more loved than i,
                your touch
                has always been hers.

the difference here is that i was not given
    the curse of a pomegranate, instead
the pain of men: forever falling prey to their transmisogyny
    the test of their desire & consumption,
a shadow of her,
    made jealous of her:
          loving you was never part of this game.
              o ambiguous hades: why not i?

monstrous bodies

monstrous body restrained
by desire & disgust
here for some time &
gone for too long.
crack maw // scatter claw
& bone;
she's dead & you alive.
alone.
alright.

FOUR

the seven sacred ways of healing

/let it out/

releasing only
as much as i thought
they could hold,
forgot NDN trans women bore
this world & watched
her die. forgot mothers
do that too.

/don't ask why/

/let it out/
/let it out/

tear through
rawing throat,
saliva & blood
bubbling
wild prairie fire
cacophony.

/there will never be an answer/

/let it out/
/let it out/
/let it out/

her hand presses
deep into my breast,
pinpointed compression
my chest billows

/tell them what they did/

                                                            /let it out/
                                                            /let it out/
                                                            /let it out/
                                                            /let it out/

my head thrown back
screams ripping out of my throat
faster than i can breathe,
my eyes strained—
hemorrhage spread
across my sclera.

                    /you will never get to ask why/

                                                            /let it out/
                                                            /let it out/
                                                            /let it out/
                                                            /let it out/
                                                            /let it out/

i cough blood &
retch, i am told
i am letting go.

                    /tell them what they did/

                                                            /let it out/
                                                            /let it out/
                                                            /let it out/
                                                            /let it out/
                                                            /let it out/
                                                            /let it out/

i can no longer lift
my arms, zhigaag takes
my place punching the bag,
our screams synchronizing,
letting go breaks everything

/this will follow them/

/let it out/
/let it out/
/let it out/
/let it out/
/let it out/
/let it out/
/let it out/
/let it out/

final screams
dying with vocal fry
& tears tinged red,
ribbon skirt pooling
around my crumpled form
hands clawing at chest
zhigaag's screams billow out now.

/they will know what it meant/

orality

i. *learned a* *t r i c k* *online:*

acupressure
to reduce my gag reflex
so i can brush my teeth properly—
get the back of my tongue
& scrub.

had to do this
because someone in an all-red tracksuit
took it too far,
couldn't hear
the *no* at the back of my throat.

too scared to sing
leave space between

tongue & tooth;

melodies fragile & spiderwebbed already.

ii. *scrub. scrub. scrub.*

maybe this mouth full of blood
a tooth will wiggle free
& i will make a fine garden
where i plant this molar.
burst from soil & gum
prairie fire.

iii.   *make a fist with thumb pressed inside*

index finger on the chin
count to five.

one   -   two   -   three   -   four   -   five
   let go.

with the hand that was clenched
pinch the other hand
 at the purlicue
count to five.

one   -   two   -   three   -   four   -   five
   let go.

iv.   *i too often forget screaming is a type of singing*

remember this while i scrub the back of my tongue.

healing // sacrifice // necessity

saltwater brine　　&　　pine-needle poultice
　　　　on fresh flesh wound where the knife bit
&　　silver needle binding angry red back together,
　　　　　　clenched teeth biting down on hardened leather
sage ash　　&　　red clay smeared on my face
　　　　tears streaking.

reopen old wounds to drain decade-old poison
　　　　&　　use traditional medicine to heal
　　　　these adhesions, abrasions　　&　　bruises;
　　　　　　grow hair out to braid in sweetgrass　　&　　twigs,
use creek-cool clay
　　　　to set fragmented & fractured bones,
　　　　　　lay tobacco tie after tobacco tie down,
　　　　　　　　i am worth every single one, my healing is worth
every prayer, every song, every ceremony.

sage lit　　&　　smoke lingering: swirling embers
　　　　carried on seaward breezes, the scent
　　　　　　sweet　　&　　pungent, the ancestors call to me
　　　　　　　　through the smoke,　　　　this controlled burn
will bring about new old-growth forest
　　　　　　soon enough.

there is a sacredness in cutting old hurt out
　　　　a sanctity in naming *it*,　　the ways i've been taken,
　　　　　　a sacrifice holding *it*, gently　　&　　firmly:
the old ways always lead us to new ways
　　　　new waters,　　new healings,　　new learnings.
it hurts in the moment,
　　　　but feeling uncomfortable

is a necessary part of growing.

i shed my clothes now, walk tentatively through the cold
    my bare feet leave footprints on the wet sand, the waves
        pulling at the shore, the bonfire heat to my exposed back,
        the darkness of the ocean calling out
the drums   &   low growl of their song pushing me
          further into the vastness of the saltwater depth.

wading into the coolness, sharp burning across
        my naked breast as i drift into *her*
    we've done this so many times before\
          &   now *her* touch lingers.

ash, clay & blood leaking into *her*   &   *she* is soaking into me
    this   //healing//hurts more than the pattern of previous takings
        the grip of *her* is seductive   &   i needn't want to leave

they come for me, rip me back to shore
        return me to the fire, smoke clinging to all parts of me
          & i let the fire wrap around my pallid & obvious flesh,
      feel my hair go up in an acrid salt blaze,
the nerves in my fingers reverberate for the first time in years
      feel myself for the first time in a long while
            feel myself leaving:
              one last & final taking.

out of necessity i burn.
    out of necessity i am taken.

waterways

i am from people made of water   &
                                    blood mixing with fermentation
        &   rich soil. i am from melding waterways
                        &   entangled red willow root system.
        on occasion, prairie storm bursts lightning-touch upon our flesh,
igniting the marshlands, sending charcoal-rich nutrients deep back into
the lands.

i learn from the waters:
        how to crack open my flesh to allow fermentation to ignite, catching
quickly to return what needs to be returned.
                i have not always tried to imitate the water of my land.

i have tried to allow my body to breach like tide on stone shores.
        chased down saltier representations of who i was ancestrally,
                never realizing my bodies have never passed these waters,
                        never had paddles caress these waves and these ways.

trans woman bodies are the ones speckled across the mixed-blood lands,
        colonially unnamed but ancestrally aplenty
                interspersed between treaty lands
                        where my great-great-grandparents
                                sold their treaty rights
                        for a slice of land to farm,
                        or a boat to fish.

last summer cousin al promises me pickerel,
        says he will feed me the cheek first, shower me in whitefish
                &   treaty card gas prices.
        al takes me on an ATV ride on the rez,
        my hands clasping too tight as the wind

whips through my messy hair
        the marsh birds crying out in distaste of this rez queer showing
the city NDN queer what the land holds.
they drive us to the river in the bed of skunk's black pickup truck;
    the kid cousins show me where the safest places are to swim
        &   where the currents would take me.
                    a muskrat tells us we are too close to her den.
these waters feel like what i imagine hugging my mother
        would feel like now:
            a long time coming—
            space missing somewhere in the middle.

a woman at the camp teaches us how to fillet pickerel,
    how to eat the cheeks.
        she tells us that her parents' generation used to be fishers,
    my great-grandparents also, but they weren't allowed to eat pickerel,
                        that was for the missionaries
            &   the day school staff.
        they were allowed to only eat the bottom dwellers,
        sucker fish.
                as she hands me the knife to slice the whitefish,
        she smiles   &   tells me that they would eat the
mud-feeder fish until the white people no longer wanted pickerel.

    i wish i were a small body of water up north by swan lake
    east of keeseekoose,
        or maybe shy of lake winnipegosis west of skownan.
        any of these vast marsh waterways would do to return to the
murky silt that continues to birth prairie storms like monstrous giants
    crashing down on flat horizons.

sometimes i use my body as a map
       trace the migration of my kin:
in the crook of my elbow is st. ambroise,
where the ducharme siblings burst from soil
      &   soft birch shoreline.
my shoulder is where regina has dug deep, having fled dauphin years prior.

    my auntie tells me i am my mother now;
       i carry her in the pocket of flesh where home should be
the dull blade of provincial child welfare carved it out over two
decades ago.

my lower abdomen is displacement
    a spiritual abruption.   wombless restlessness buckles
      beneath fat in the place where the west coast rests in my
map of kinship.

my hormone-fuelled shifting body
    lets me unlearn muscle memories
        by allowing myself to touch my tender breasts
         &   rewild my once-forbidden intimacies.

in skownan, an auntie tells me about my great-grandmother.
        it is a different story from the rest, i am told.
     a young man ran to her house
with freshly picked rhubarb   &   strawberries
   asking her to make a pie for his sweetheart.
that evening my great-grandmother crossed the reserve
                by foot to deliver the pie
    made with love   &   kinship.

i sometimes wish i could've tried it,
    tasted the rich juices   &   felt my teeth plunge
        into the sweet flesh of the heartberries   &   rhubarb.

i am cracking open.
    the water in me pooling in preparation.
        i can feel this west coast colonially queer community sneer
as i beg for matchstick relief.

non-prairie folk
        do not understand that burning down does not mean the end.
oftentimes when we prairie marshlanders rise from the blackened mud
        we are the monsters of nightmares
without them ever realizing we had ensured the health of the land
        &   our people.

in eurocentric queer communities
        trans women are the first to burn
a tempting end, how delicious it would be to watch my flesh sizzle
    off bone   &   catch the vancouver community ablaze—
        if the burning flesh of trans women
        is enough to destroy a movement or space or collective
what does this say about them?

i try to not burst into terrifying blaze
    around anyone who cannot handle it.
        i follow the teachings of moving the water in me
to the tunes of sacred queer dance floor.
    jeffrey mcneil-seymour tells me it is dancing my trauma out.

with each hip shake   &   hair flip
       feel my body becoming loose
              witness the tight grip of concrete roadways
     sinking into the marsh of my flesh.
          recreating the waterways of the land
            that flow in my flesh
i scare off those who cling to concrete, rebar   &   tar.

when my jaw cracks open dry lightning strike
        fire pours out in unrelenting force
            burning up nerves   &   synapses alike.

no matter the hip shake or mud dip
     this body is trauma   &   trauma still needs to be excised
     the water still needs to burn.

queer//rition

my queer feels like interruption:
        a *sorry to bother you—*
            in my throat
            hard words choked down
            every sunday service.

my queer feels like abruption:
how i imagine the moon feels
sometimes about nimama aki
the separation   of the placenta
from the wall of the uterus
displace   //   meant.

my queer feels like abnegation:
        beneath childhood floorboards,
                myself into existence only when i sleep—
dreams far too star filled
&   not scorched earth enough.

my queer feels like perdition:
damned if i do   //   damned if i don't
sent away to pray hard enough to see him
hope he heals the demons in my marrow;
maybe all that time on my knees
was good for me?

my queer feels like accusation:
sour milk curdled in freshly brewed coffee,
bruises tender   &   blue blossoming
on thigh   &   rib
classmates tugging down gym strip.

my queer feels like condemnation:
how often this has come about
teetering at sidewalk wondering if it ever ended
how one   small   step could finish
what so many   had started.

my queer feels like redaction:
erased from the history books,
people like me in dog pits
&   burned alive—
my grade nine social studies teacher tells me
the winners
                will always write our history books.

my queer feels like contradiction:
a collision of queries,
wonder if i was right to say *no*   all those years ago,
or if maybe,   if i had said *yes*
maybe   i would've been happier?

//

my queer feels now like decolonization:
sweetgrass bound by root   &   aki
singing the parts of the song i want to—
sacred sweat,   crying out for nimama,
have her hold my face one last time.

my queer feels now like celebration:
something worth living for
or at least fighting hard enough for—
held together by multitude   under flashing lights
many hands   &   many hearts.

my queer feels now like salvation:
i broke vow   &   testimony
allowed thirsty mouths upon my breast—
realized we didn't have to cry   on sundays any longer
came to understand i was only ever
                                        interrupting myself.

raven

the raven returned
        carrying the sunset
                on their wings

pulling the wind
        through the long grass
                of the plains

the raven returned
        when the children
                awoke

their bodies milk
        hungry smelling
                of freshly crushed cinnamon

the raven returned
        our languages
                of love

love that raised the grass
        invited the children
                into existence

love that brought
        sage, cedar, salt
                &   tobacco back

the raven returned
        as the wild strawberries ripened
                across the sunset plains

sweetgrass dancing
      with the children
            born from the sweat lodge

the raven returned
      these young ones
            with song   &   dance

words never heard before
      ceremony in their souls
            crying with laughter

the raven returned
      having heard the music
            the song   &   dance

the children's faces
      sticky from strawberries
            their tummies filled

the raven returned
      one early evening
            croaked a hello

saltwater ocean cleansing
            the wounds of old

the raven returned
      bringing with them
            dreams of tomorrow

futures built by the children
      their laughter   &   love

the raven returned
      the call of the ceremonies

the raven returned
      the call of the children

           the raven returns.

about the ones i want to love

when i planted my heart in the corner of the yard,
        by the strawberries and rhubarb:
           what did i expect to happen?

what did i expect
    to happen when i tried to love   &
        my heart was buried ten years ago
      by a house that was never home?

       i want to go back now
i hear the garden was pulled up
    stripped from the willing   &   giving soil
      for strawberries   &   rhubarb were too much trouble
          for her at her old age.

i wonder if my heart was unearthed
thrown into the forest behind the house with the rest of the compost
i wonder if some strawberry plants resisted her pull & still come up
    through grass
      or if some took root in the compost pile
      &   have crept down the ravine's edge.

a delicious half-breed settler in indigenous foliage.
    i wonder if the bear cubs feast
      on plump red berries & juices as an act of resistance.

i wonder if they feasted on my heart?
    you see, i wouldn't mind that
      i had gotten used to sharp teeth on my heart
      before i cut her out of my chest
        i even had to break a few bones to do it.

but if a cub ate my heart to grow up strong,
                                    then i am at peace with that.

                        /but/

if not
        i would like to dig her up
            break the bones in my chest again
                sew her back in
        with red   &   silver thread   &   wooden beads
            patch together with ribbons   &   cedar.
        i would set the bones with ash   &   clay.

it will hurt more:
        for scar tissue is protection   &   thickness
                rough   &   tough
                        the body saying *not again*
                            scar tissue covers nerves
                                            &   you have to cut
                            a little deeper to get
                                to where you want.

this is my fault
            no longer wanting to be a wandering ghost
                    in a community of other healing beings.

what did i expect
            when i found people with hearts mending
                & they handed me a chance
                        to hold their heart for a moment?
what did i expect
        when i came face to face with my people
            for the first time in my existence

what did i expect
    when for once in my life touch doesn't have to be flinch?

what did i expect
    when i heard the cherry tree   &   apple tree
        got root rot,
            died shortly after i left?
    when the guilt of burying such a precious thing
        under such carelessly nurtured fruit trees.

what did i expect
      when every plant
          that ever provided
              for the inhabitants of the house ceased
                  to exist after i left?

i buried my heart in hopes my heart would be
            enough to keep them fed in the winter

/but/

i see that sacrifice failed
    ultimately i want her back now
        i want to give more than just half-empty words
                to the ones i want to love,
    it is not fair for me to be such a living ghost
        who can come   &   go as i please
    all whilst holding their heart in the palm of my hand.

so now
    i cleanse my body
        mark where i am to cut
            prepare the herbs and tools,

get ready to exhume her from her tomb

healing is sacred   &   i want to love   &   be alive again.

it's time.
    been time for too long now.

can you hear that?

//thud thud/—/thud thud/—/thud thud//

//thud thud/—/thud thud/—/thud thud//
    //thud thud/—/thud thud/—/thud thud//
      //thud thud/—/thud thud/—/thud thud//
    //thud thud/—/thud thud/—/thud thud//   *//thud thud/—/thud thud/—/thud thud////thud thud/—/thud thud/—/thud thud//*

    //thud thud/—/thud thud/—/thud thud//   *//thud thud/—/thud thud/—/thud thud//*   *//thud thud/—/thud thud/—/thud thud////thud thud/—/thud thud/—/thud thud////thud thud/—/thud thud/—/thud thud//*

    //thud thud/—/thud thud/—/thud thud// //thud thud/—/thud thud/—/thud thud////thud thud/—/thud thud/—/thud thud//
    //thud thud/—/thud thud/—/thud thud////thud thud/—/thud thud/—/thud thud////thud thud/—/thud thud/—/thud thud////thud thud/—/thud thud/—/thud thud////thud thud/—/thud thud/—/thud thud////thud thud/—/thud thud/—/thud thud////thud thud/—/thud thud/—/thud thud////thud thud/—/thud thud/—/thud thud////thud thud/—/thud thud/—/thud thud////thud thud/—/thud thud/—/thud thud////thud thud/—/thud thud/—/thud thud////thud thud/—/thud thud/—/thud thud////thud thud/—/thud thud/—/thud thud////thud thud/—/thud thud/—/thud thud////thud thud/—/

thud thud/—/thud thud////thud thud/—/thud thud/—/thud thud////
thud thud/—/thud thud/—/thud thud////thud thud/—/thud thud/—/
thud thud////thud thud/—/thud thud/—/thud thud////thud thud/—/
thud thud/—/thud thud////thud thud/—/thud thud/—/thud thud////
thud thud/—/thud thud/—/thud thud////thud thud/—/thud thud/—/
thud thud////thud thud/—/thud thud/—/thud thud////thud thud/—/
thud thud/—/thud thud//

let's begin.

notes

"the end of a friendship" borrows lyrics from Florence + the Machine's "Big God" from their fourth studio album *High as Hope* (2018).

"loving in the dark" is after Amy Winehouse's "Tears Dry on Their Own" from her second studio album *Back to Black* (2006).

"*norman fucking rockwell!* is lana del rey's greatest album" is titled after Lana Del Rey's sixth studio album *Norman Fucking Rockwell!* (2019).

"bedroom hymns" borrows lyrics and its title from Florence + the Machine's second studio album *Ceremonials Deluxe Edition* (2011).

"in a city without seasons…" borrows lyrics and is titled from Florence + the Machine's "Sky Full of Song" on their fourth studio album *High as Hope* (2018).

"godzilla" references the Legendary Pictures film *Godzilla* (2014).

acknowledgements

Earlier versions of select poems can be found at:

Poetry Is Dead Magazine — "healing//sacrifice//necessity" (Spring 2018)
THIS Magazine — "this woman//nookum" (Fall 2018)
PRISM international — "the raven returned" (Fall 2018)
Room Magazine — "the seven sacred ways of healing" (Spring 2019)
Grain Magazine — "decolonial pu$$y" (Summer 2019)
Grain Magazine — "bedroom hymns" (Summer 2019)
Hustling Verse: An Anthology of Sex Workers' Poetry — "godzilla" (Fall 2019)
Hustling Verse: An Anthology of Sex Workers' Poetry — "r e d" (Fall 2019)
Burnaby Art Gallery's *Echo Exhibition* — "w a t e r w a y s" (Winter 2019)
GUTS Magazine — "Urban NDNs in the DTES" (Spring 2020)

To Silas, Carleton and Emma at Nightwood Editions: Miigwech for holding this collection of vulnerability and allowing my voice and story a conduit.

To Angela: Miigwech for bringing *it was never going to be okay*'s cover to life with vibrant lushness.

To the Canada Council of the Arts: I wouldn't have been able to take the time necessary to tend the flame of this work without support of the Explore and Create grant.

To Emily and Jessica: The kinship and generosity you've both gifted me has allowed reprieve and growth over these two adventurous years. Miigwech Emily for your help with my very messy Cree.

To Arielle: Your sisterhood has saved me more times than I can count. No expanse of land can keep us apart.

To Evan, Justin, Brandi and Joshua: From Manitoba mud we were made, through our fires we were freed.

To Billy-Ray: I never thought I would have a GBF, but here you are, the Trixie to my Katya.

To Sara & Kathleen: My favourite clowns whom I owe at least a few dinners at the Keg.

To Jillian, Amber Dawn, Dina, Ben, Daniel and Mairi: Your belief in me throughout the years kept me from giving up many times.

To Jen and David: May the bridges we burn light the way.

To Marcelo: I've never known a love like this. Miigwech for putting up with listening to the same song over and over and over again. Zaagi'giin.

To my Banff babes: Canisia, Chimwemwe, Cooper, Lou, Nicole, Leslie, Sanna, Aaron and Natasha: remember a group of poets is a ruckus and a kindness. May the Mountain Goats thrive, and the Earth remain round.

To Robert, Carolynn, Betty, Majlinda, Cindy, Mary-Ellen and Chris: You all told me I was more than just a foster kid. You told me I was worthy of love, justice and peace.

To Mark, Peter, Grandma Flo, nimama and the many others I wasn't allowed to mourn: We had the briefest of times together but you all have home in my heart.

To the many who believed in me: Azucena, Terria, Jade F, Jenna, John, Cate, Kayleigh, Patricia, Jaime, Karmella, Steven, Destiny, Alicia, Cherie, Jennifer Alicia, Em & Ev, Lindsay, Lacie & Bee, Edzi'u, Aurora, Estiqw & Oliver, Valeen, Heather, Sii-am, Whess, Kalilah, Ta'Kaiya, Richard, Jade B,

Ziibiwan, Deo, Kiara, Jess B, Kris, Hiromi, Khalid, RJ, Marielle, Brett, Emily O, Jonina, Shaheed, Andrea, Rach, Daven, Danny, Zachary, Morgan, !Kona, Jeffrey, Brianna, Allie, Schuyler, Sarah, Selina, Adrienne, Autumn, Charlotte, Naheed, Tyler, Matt, Savannah & Jam, Sue, Donald, Brent and so many more.

To the many who took without abandon: I grant you no absolution.

To my NDN kin in care: You are so much more than they'll ever know.

To nîtisânak: We deserved so much more than what we were given

PHOTO CREDIT: DIVYA NANRAY, 2019

about the author

jaye simpson is an Oji-Cree Saulteaux Indigiqueer writer and activist from the Sapotaweyak Cree Nation, with Scottish and French settler ancestry. Their poems and essays are published in *Poetry Is Dead, THIS Magazine, PRISM international, SAD Magazine, GUTS Magazine, Room, Today's Parent, Grain,* and *SubTerrain*. simpson is also published in *Hustling Verse: An Anthology of Sex Workers' Poetry,* as well as *Love After the End: An Anthology of Two-Spirit and Indigiqueer Speculative Fiction*. simpson is currently resisting, ruminating and residing on xʷməθkʷəy̓əm (Musqueam), səl̓ilwətaʔł (Tsleil-waututh), and sḵwx̱wú7mesh (Squamish) First Nations territories, colonially known as Vancouver. *it was never going to be okay* is their first book.